bleed

mia laurén
herrera

For my mom,
even the most angelic poem
will never be able to capture
you.

For the seventeen
and for every other innocent person
who walked into a war zone
when they should have been walking into a school.

del•ic•i•ae

noun
feminine (substantive), vocative, plural

translation from latin
1. beloved
2. dear one

You are my *deliciae*.

Poetry is not a monologue.
It is a conversation.

Hello.

You.
Yes, *deliciae,*
I am speaking to you.

I need you to break.

> Break without boundaries.
> Break irreversibly.
> Break because it will enable you
> to love and to live again.

Can you do that for me?

bleed

I need to wash my hands,
so I can be clean.

    Not of my sins,
    but of yours.

Are they 'out of your league?'
Do they bleed gold?

bleed

The things I'll never tell
will not be a laundry list of my regrets.

I will bear myself to you voluntarily
because I have nightmares of dying
with words still in my throat,
with poems still in my veins,
with love still in my heart.

When I die,
I will have said everything
there is to say.

One day you will realize
you are in the center of the life
you have dreamt of for so long.

I hope it is everything you imagined
    and if it isn't,
      I hope you keep dreaming.

It is much more interesting
to say a person is profound
in an abundance of microscopic ways,
than to say a person
is overwhelmingly ordinary.

**Are you comfortable
trapped inside that box of stereotypes**
that is carved into your skin,
but absent from your heart?

bleed

You hate the people who broke you.
You hate them with all that you are.

Then,
you look into the mirror,
        and somehow,
there they are.

Take a pen to paper,
bleed.

I share my mind
so we might realize
**we are more alike
than we ever could have imagined.**

When we first met
I had no clue
you would one day
become my air.

You see
    these chains
    weighing down my desire to jump,

    this narrow path
    I cannot veer from,

    these Words
    painted on my skin.

You see these things
and you think I am trapped.

Look further.
Look deeper.
Take a microscope to my soul.

**These are the only barriers
protecting me
from myself.**

This is not a reckless freedom,
but a freedom of love.

Is it such a bad thing
that I revert to language when I am lost?

    Collapsing into words
    is the only barrier preventing me
    from collapsing into darkness.

Unappealing art is hard to witness
because it takes our view of the world
and obliterates it.

How many more lives do we have to lose
before we acknowledge
      that hate does not diffuse hate,
      that loving those
      who are brutally and wickedly broken
      is the only way to restore
      the humanity inside of them?

Look at me.
    Not like that.

Stare at my soul.

    Now,
    tell me
    I am worth nothing.

Write to heal others,
not to tear them down.

Even when people turn vile,
remind them
they still have worth.

Why, you ask,
should I try to fix the damaged?

Wasn't it words that put you back together
when you couldn't bear to think about
the atrocities you have committed?

bleed

Becoming an adult
takes as long as it takes,
even if your soul
is centuries older
than your body.

You look at me
and see one being,
but this is not so.

    I am my grandma's laugh,
    my dad's afflictions,
    my aunt's grief.

You see one,
but I am hundreds of people.

bleed

As I stood gazing at the mountains,
I came to the understanding
of the connection between us.

Every time I glance at the tall landmark,
I find that the changing colors
say everything my pen cannot.
The mountains are a canvas.

What perplexes me though,
is how the Painter hears my unwritten words
and puts them on display
for the entire city to fawn over.

It's alright
to be consumed
every now and then.

bleed

Truth whispers in my ear every night,
softly humming over the sound
of pages turning and
white noise whispering voiceless.

In the morning you ask me
how I know.

Am I to explain Wisdom itself?

You love
and you have been loved,
but still you are empty.

Perhaps you have not been loved
by the right person.

Or perhaps, *deliciae,*
the only right person is
you.

A catastrophe doesn't have to strike
for you to tell them how you feel.

**'I love you' is the one phrase
that shouldn't be said out of desperation
when the world caves in on itself.**

It should be the only truth that doesn't tremble.

Don't try to cover my poems with flowers
to extract the blood from these words.

These poems could soak through every white petal
and still have more to drip.

Poetry stains.
Let it.

Put that flag back down.

Half-staff will suffice for the murdered children,
and the hundreds before them.
They don't rise from their graves
when the flag returns to its summit.

Keep the flags at half
until children and teachers
are not being shot in schools.
Keep them down for weeks,
for months,
for years,
if that is what it will take.

And when we rise
with our voices carrying
the ones who have been stolen from us,
then and only then
can the flags rise again.

How do we fight a war
when the enemy is one of us?

The struggles this country carries
are so much larger
than a difference of opinion
or a single person's bigotry.

This cracking of our foundations
is hardly political.

This is about restoring soul.

The world is filled
with too many broken children
because their parents don't know how to love.

It is criminal
to have a sweltering passion
and suppress it
breathless.

How are you still breathing
with those words stuck in your throat?

The next time someone asks you
how you are doing,
I need you to free yourself.

Tell them how incredibly painful it is
to keep saying
you are good
when you are splintering.

bleed

Say it.

I live for gentle mornings.

The ones that have a pink haze over them.
The mornings that taste like home.
When God turns the sky into a canvas.

It is okay
if you need
to put the pen down for a while,
if you need
a breath of air not made up of words.

**It is okay
to take off the heart of a poet**
and remember what it is like
to feel in moderation again.

**Religion is the color
we don't wear on our skin.**

It deserves respect.
It holds weight.

bleed

You do not have to
set your life ablaze
to be a poet.

Just your heart will do.

You know,
that one poem.

The one that never fails
to knock the breath out of your lungs?

That is what you were to me.

bleed

If after all this,
the only thing I have is memories,
I regret nothing.

To the boy who I saw, but never knew,

I am sorry my memory of you is so limited.
You were a shadow
in an already blurry childhood.

I have absentmindedly carried you all these years,
keeping you tucked away in my catalog of faces,
until you twisted my arm,
giving me no choice,
but to remember.

In the courtyard,
among the other kids,
I saw you smiling
the smile of an angel.

That's it.
That is my only recollection of you
living.
Not that I saw you dead.

It was a closed casket,
your funeral.
I went to your funeral.

I went
to your funeral
because for some inexplicable reason
the image of your smile
has stayed will me all this time.

What happened
between those two memories of you?
What changed you
from the boy with
the most genuine smile
to the boy being carried down the aisle in a box?

The sun existed just for you that day.
It was your spotlight,
and I was your audience.
You put on the most captivating show
the world has ever seen,
except the world was not invited,
just me.

I was perfectly fine
forgetting about you.

I was perfectly fine
letting you slip from my mind.

I was perfectly fine
never thinking about your smile,
or your spotlight,
or your authenticity.

I sobbed at your funeral.

Your beautiful show
is branded into my brain,
next to your tragic ending.

To the boy who I saw, but never knew,

I feel like I should say goodbye,
but how can I do that
when I never even said
hello.

bleed

How can I feel this much
for someone
I didn't know?

Trying to kill one addiction with another
is like trying to escape the heat of the sun
by running towards it.

bleed

These are the days
we are going to remember.

Can't you hear
our future selves
calling out to us
to breathe it all in?

> The love in our eyes.
> The laughter in our hearts.
> The friendship of our souls.

First,
before we talk about
violence and hate,
let's infuse our voices with love.

Imagine the possibilities
if our first reaction to evil
was to submerge ourselves,
was submerge the world,
was to submerge the very evil itself
in love.

bleed

If the only thing
keeping you in a relationship
is the fear of being abandoned,
deliciae,
you are already alone.

I have ripped myself open
and stained these papers red
hoping you will realize
**there are words
blocking your blood flow too.**

bleed

We live for the moments
when we spill the contents of our hearts
into the hands of another.

But what if
the most powerful words
are the ones we do not pour out?

What if
the most powerful words
are the ones we never say?

Allow breaking.

Follow profoundly
what mends you.

My soul cannot bear
to hear the bullet holes
in her words
once more.

Beauty hurts,
I was told

      as my face was being plucked at,
      and my hair was being tied back so tightly
      I could barely see out of my own eyes,
      and I wailed to go back to my sandbox
      in the backyard underneath the swing set.

Beauty should not hurt.

      It should be gentle,
      serene.

Beauty is the smell of the first day of spring.
It is the eye of the storm.

Or perhaps,
beauty is the storm itself.

Write it down.

Now you are free to
let it go.

Relationships should add to your identity,
not make it disappear.

bleed

Know that I am okay
even if my poems
make you think
the cracks in my veins
cannot be glued back together.

When I stop writing,
    that is when you should be
    checking my pulse.

They are galaxies apart,
    when you leave
    and when you are being left.

Listen to the whisper in your ear
telling you to take in
everything there is to take in
because
    this mending
    this feeling
    this cracking
is living.

I haven't thought about you in a thousand lifetimes.

After all these years between us,
you, in my mind again,
seem too far away to be real
and too faint to wrap my arms around you
to welcome home.

**There are many who can craft words
much better than I.**

I am in constant envy of these people.
I would also never have a dream without them.

I wonder how many versions of myself
I have killed
by starving my bones
of the opportunity to dream.

When you look in the mirror
whose reflection do you see?

Yours?

Or the things
that have devoured you?

I do not say anything
when you dislodge my spine from my body
with your jokes.

I keep from spewing years
of built up anger at you,
but my soul is cutting itself
trying to scrape away
every wound you have inflicted.

This silence that I have forced myself into
is literally killing me,
is literally making me
kill myself.

Every now and then,
a poem won't need the assistance of a pen.

Trust these poems.

> They are ready,
> even if the world
> isn't quite ready for them.

How many heartbeats are you willing to spend in vain?

You may have to splinter,
so you can
collapse into yourself.

Be inspired.

    Find beauty in the familiar.

    In the unique pattern of the leaves.
    In the water that engulfs you,
    starting with your toes,
    then consuming your soul.

Listen to the bird's song.
Fall into the traffic's flow.
Take in the perplexity of the city late at night.

Feel the gentle breeze.
Hear the hum of God.

bleed

What would it mean
if the coincidence that reshaped your life
wasn't a coincidence at all?

If you share your soul with someone,
they become a safe haven,
**a place to be whoever you need to be
in order to continue on.**

bleed

Please, travel.
By all means, go explore.

Absorb the world into your skin,
but do not think that
a change of scenery
erases everything,
or changes anything,
about you.

I have to ask.

Did you think of me
when you beat me beyond recognition
just because you knew
I had never been to hell before?

Did you think of me?

I hope so
because it seems
like a monstrous thing to do,
        to break my life into fragments
        and not even have the manners
        to hold the door open,
        so that my soul
        could leave with some respect.

Take back your life.
It was never theirs to steal.

Each time you held your pen
and wrote nothing
     was equally important,
     if not more,
     to the times you wrote
     an entire world into existence.

Normal never did anything for anyone.
Normal isn't outraged.

It doesn't scream.

The problem with this country
is that we have lost our sense of the poetic.

**Imagine a world where every person
is viewed as a poem.**

There would be a surmounting symphony of pens
filling in the cracks of humanity
we have so tragically broken.

bleed

Are you truly that wholesome,
        to look at someone
        and believe you are worth more?

No amount
        of money,
        of goodness,
        of privilege,
will ever make one human
rise above another.

I am living the life
my great grandparents envisioned
when they longed to speak English,
only to hear the snap
of a ruler against their knuckles,

when they felt the heat of the sun
soaking into their skin, yet again,

when every muscle in their body needed to rest,
but something inside of them pleaded to keep moving,

when they looked up at the stars at two in the morning
and wondered why things are they way they are.

Little did they know that
I was that pleading voice
and I was that star.

> My ancestors and I
> have been communicating
> for centuries now.

It has taken me all of these years to realize that
I am carrying entire generations on my shoulders.

I am everything they could never be.

bleed

Deliciae, your heart stays with you
regardless of how much you wish
a new one would grow
out of the guilt-ridden ashes
of your soul.

When the world starts cracking,
the only option is to pray
that the people who said
'I love you'
still have those words
lingering in every breath.

It is made out to be magical,
    being a poet.

Yes, I agree,
it can be quite extraordinary,
but it is not exclusive.

Here,
take a pen.

Join me.

If your heart is smiling,
I urge you
to breathe in
the world's wonders.

And when you find
that darkness is creeping in,
I urge you
to fall into poetry
and let yourself shatter.

bleed

There comes a time
when you must decide
to stop bearing others' burdens.

Finally, I understand
why losing you was so excruciating.

Before, when friends have left,
it was like getting a haircut.

      But when you left,
      every single bone in my body
      was amputated.

In your absence,
I don't feel whole,
and that is because you
literally
left me in pieces.

bleed

Would you believe me if I told you
your soul could breathe again
if anger wasn't tucking you in at night?

I am finally trying to soak up
the language my ancestors
are shouting for me to understand,
but it has been washed from my tongue
in the same way a rainstorm
wipes away a broken heart.

But this stripping of language,
this destroying of history,
this flogging of my culture,
is not a cleansing
of any sorts.

This is murder.

It was in that moment
they let each other go,
and it was in that moment
they sold the best versions
of their futures away.

I long for the person I could have been
if I had never endured
what I have endured.

But without these rips in my soul
I would not have experienced
    this grace,
    this peace,
    this love,
    this mercy.

Perseverance has two sides.

Even if our love fades,
    it will sing songs
    long past the time
    we stop writing music.

I can hear you telling me
that one word cannot be
an entire poem.

Love.

Is that not the most
profound poem
humanity has ever written?

bleed

Peace either becomes you,
    or it is the voice in the wind.

I do not have time to write, I say.

Since when has breathing
been optional?

I looked at my hands today.

**You have erased my fingerprints
and penciled in your own.**

I must be a heavy sleeper,
      to not notice such a change.

Acquiring wisdom consists of a lifetime of monumental misdirections.

bleed

Even the clouds cry
when the weight they are holding is too heavy.

They scream out all of their anger
and let the past fall.

They move on knowing
this showering of emotion
will come and go again tomorrow.

You are strong, *deliciae,*
but not more so than the clouds.

Don't try to be.

**Every Sunday
I come back to you.**

Humbly,
softly,
with my heart
in my hand,

I return home once again.

The tears you hold back
are the ones you should fear the most.

Bigger isn't always better.

The small moments are the ones that stay.
Small poems change the world.

Small prayers?
Well, they hold the most truth.

Poetry is less
    about being the author
    of an epiphany
and more
    about taking heed
    when it doesn't seem like
    there is anything to look at.

You
are not
the first thing
that should come to mind
when I look at
myself.

My spine splits my body and my spirit into two.

How am I supposed to walk
when one foot wants to go forward
and the other backward?

How am I supposed to speak
when half of my tongue knows one language,
and the other half stays silent
because it is trying to learn a language
from the voices of my ancestors?

How am I supposed to go home
when my body pulls me in two directions?

  The first, toward the road
  that immerses me in euphoric memories
  of my seamless, yet fleeting childhood.

  The second, toward the road
  that looks like success,
  but holds so many broken days
  and even more wretched nights.

How am I supposed to live
when I contradict myself
just by breathing?

In a crowd of protesters,
there is a red anger,
a demanding anger,
and hopefully
an anger so genuine
and so peaceful,
it glows.

My poems are stained
by the flowers singing
in your lungs.

It is okay if a poem
didn't walk up and greet you today.

It is probably stuck in traffic.

Please.
Please stay.
Please, just stay.
I need you.
The world needs you.
If you cannot stay for yourself,
stay for me.

Okay?
Deliciae.
Beloved.
Most loved.

Stay for me.
Stay for me long enough
that you find value in being alive again
and you breathe on your own
and you pump your own blood.

But until then,
let me.
Let me be your life support.

You are not alone.
Can you feel my soul hugging yours?

bleed

I have never said
you must agree with me,
only that you have to respect
what I believe.

And yet,
here you stand
reaching down my throat,
clenching my heart with your fist,
and heaving out
the spine of my soul.

I do not stand on a foundation of inconsistency.

If I were to write a thousand poems
that nobody would ever read,
would they still matter?

Yes.

For so many reasons,
yes.

Once more I sit down to write,
and again the empty page prevails.

It is hard to decipher nothingness from creativity
that is so fervent, it leaves the writer speechless.

You must crave a life that holds meaning
over one that holds nothing but itself
if you ever want to change.

How many deaths
take place inside of a person

  for them to touch their own skin
  and feel as if a monster was grabbing hold,

  to stare into their own eyes
  and see nothing?

**Explain to me
how a person can look at their own life
and think it has no worth.**

Explain to me
because I don't understand
how a person can put up so many walls
that they don't see
how desperately
they are needed
and how desperately
they are wanted
and how the world
truly
will not go on
without them.

The sky
cries and shines and sulks,
is blue and gray and pink,
is blown by wind,
and is still
all at the same time.

I have never found a better metaphor
to explain myself.

Take me back to the nights
when we hesitated to go to sleep,
fearing that moments like this
would run away with the moon.

Stop saying this world is doomed.
Stop talking about hell on earth.

I have to live in this world.
I have to raise my kids here.

I have to search
for beauty among devastation.

I have to find love
here.

**Never be tricked into thinking
you only regret that which you do not do.**

It is not the missed moments
that will haunt you,
but the tangible memories
when Evil squeezed your heart
and drowned it in black.

When I was a kid,
I used to be excited for summer
because of lazy mornings,
wrinkly fingers from too much time in the pool,
and never-ending tubs of ice cream.

Now I am excited for summer
because for just a few months
there isn't a target on my back
    because I carry books
    and write essays
    and take tests.

People question
how children lose their innocence.

    This is how.

Stop beating yourself up.

I can hold your fists down,
if you need me to.

I can tell you that it's okay,
if you need me to.
I might be lying,
but isn't it comforting
to entertain the idea of tranquility
just for a second?

Unclench your fists, *deliciae.*
Rest.

I want every poem to grab my hand
and make me feel at home
so when it rips truth,
I am
        speechless.

You insist there is no magic
left inside of you
but how,

    when our past
    has disappeared from your memory
    and when your soul
    teleports in and out of your body.

**You are the greatest magician
I have ever known.**

bleed

I don't want to hear stories that leave me
the same as they found me.

I want stories that are raw,

> that tear down walls
> between good and evil,

> between borders,

> between my skin
> and my heart.

Love like a poet,
they say.

I assure you,
whoever wrote that
is not a poet
because poets know
**our love is the most breathtaking
and the most destructive**
all at once.

Why must we ruin the people
we consider to be talented?

They are talented,
but more importantly,
they are human.

Maybe,
we should let them
be human
and stop treating them
like a divine entity.

The sad thing
is that it's easier to disappear
than it is to be seen.

How many times can a person die
and walk back through the flames?

I guess
as long
as they choose to see
the allure of constantly being on fire.

Every day is glazed over in a different color.

Pink when the world
has not quite woken up yet.

Yellow for the days that
deserve a picture frame.

Orange in the times of merciful peace.

Red when a day holds too much anger
in the palm of its hand.

Green for the rejuvenation
of everything that has been lost.

Blue when the cold has sneaked
its way under your skin.

Purple for the days that are are still
raw to the touch.

Imagine how different our world would be
**if we stopped dragging
our souls across the ground
and instead threw them up
onto our shoulders.**

And let them breathe.
Let them see.
Let them out of the cage
they are hopelessly enslaved in.

There are days
when I feel like my heart
beats outside of my chest
and allows the world to warm
whatever ice was forming.

We are all human.

**This should be reason enough
to love one another,**
     don't you think?

Poetry is shaping the magical,
as well as the ordinary,
into a form that can be folded up
and carried in ones pocket.

bleed

You forgot
to wipe the blood
from your lips.

Your own tongue
is a victim of your toxic words.

Hearts don't wake up one day
and forget the people
who have carved paintings
on their walls.

These marks will never fade,
will never be erased.

And if by some incomprehensible miracle
they do disappear,
I will be the first to grab a pen
and etch them into my heart again
because I never,
not in any breath,
or after a hundred years,
or ever in my existence
want a day to go by
without you on my mind.

In the end we are all remarkably similar.
For some people this is extraordinary.
For others it is crippling.

Some words
are too evil.

Some words
could change everything.

**Some words
could take the world
in its hand
and slash it open
with a dagger**
if they were to ever fully
sink in.

bleed

Somewhere down the line
you will find the hatred that has been hiding
for the ones you once loved more than yourself
and, *deliciae*, it will destroy you.

Then one day,
when you are ready,
you will stand up
and you will walk away
and you will be free.

I do not understand
people who stay away from the cold.

There is something so beautiful
about the contradiction of a warm heart
engulfed in a freezing world,
radiating out and defrosting ice.

I don't have many answers.

I just have peace telling me that
not knowing is okay.

Would you still love me
if I had no more poems left to give?
I asked,
not knowing that her response
would always quietly
be shouting in my mind.

    Would you still love yourself
    if you were not
    constantly dreaming of words?

You wrote novels on your heart for them
and they never even opened the cover.

If this is not a sign to let them go,
I don't know if you ever will.

**You are either with a person
or you are not.**

Love him even
when he is not the person
you fell in love with.

But if you have loved him
when he is unloveable
and still,
the one you used to know
has not returned,
I will be the first to tell you
to kiss his ghost goodbye.

A wise artist knows
when a piece should be left alone
and when it should be thrown
into the world
to scream.

For once
    I want to be able to say
    that I fell into something resembling light
    instead of ritualistic darkness.

Is that all this is to you?
    The punch line of a joke.

**I ask you to be mindful when talking
about beliefs that are not your own.**

I ask you
softly
    because raising my voice
    will cause an avalanche to trap me.

I ask you
peacefully
    because I do not want to fight.

I ask you
finally
    with a weeping soul
    because you do not realize
    how you are killing me.

The words
will give you so many hearts
that you will feel like your chest is exploding.

Even so,
this will not be enough.

bleed

The insides of my eyelids
are painted with murals of you.

You insist I forget,
but every blink
draws my heart closer
to what we have lost.

Trust is blind with hope.

Faith is the one that has seen
what is unseen.

If you continue to suppress
the softness inside of you,
deliciae, you will turn into stone.

We are not afraid of you,
the people with the guns
who fire bullets of hatred,
of bigotry,
of cowardice,
into crowds
and into classrooms.

You have frozen over,
but if we,
if you,
**if anybody or if anything
could defrost you,**
oh,
      what a loving,
      what a peaceful,
      what a beautiful,
remedy that would be.

Just for a moment,
        take your heart
        out of your body
and be helplessly overwhelmed
by the insignificant.

Because we see the flag waving
and hear echoes of freedom ringing,
we call ourselves free?

In the quiet moments,
the moments that
shouldn't have been quiet,
     is when I miss you most.

**Before you are able
to put it into words,
you must feel it
in every cell of your body.**

This can take a second.
That's okay.

This can take years.
That's okay.

This may never take place at all.
You may never put it into words.

Guess what?
That's okay.

Secrecy had become so intertwined into our beings that we whispered when we were alone.

We feared a Listener who didn't have ears.

I can see the unrest
through your skin.

If you do not let this blistering anger evaporate,

it will scorch the flowers
of your soul with acid rain,

it will obliterate
any trace of tenderness,

it will turn your entire body
into ash.

Losing your beliefs
is a thousand times easier
than grabbing hold of them again.

If I write as a way to measure my worth,
I must stop.

If I write solely to satisfy others,
I must stop.

If I write because I crave language,
I will write on.

But if I write because I have to,
does that mean the words and I are a perfect match?

Or does it make me a coward
who is too afraid to live a life
without a pen in hand?

bleed

'It is snowing cotton' I say,
as my mom and I stare outside
from the living room window.

My mom whispers something I cannot quite catch.
She always makes the most profound statements
in the lowest of voices,
        like the first hint of green sprouting in spring,
        she knows what is ahead,
        but waits patiently for the rest of us
        to discover it for ourselves.

Tell me.

Is is comforting or terrifying
to know the world goes on when you die?

Maybe it's a little bit of both.

bleed

I am hopelessly clinging to the fact
that it did not happen
if I do not ink a paper with the casualties.

This, however, is only an excuse,
worn with so many bullet holes
that I can't trick myself
into believing its lies once more.

I have been waiting all day
to come home to the quietness of my room,
open my journal
and fall into it like a dream.

Time is never a guarantee.

It is the only thing
that will be with you
for your entire life,
and still leave too soon.

I am a flower.

I said this and they thought
it was a weakness,
        to be delicate.

They ripped off all of my petals,
thinking they would never grow back.

Yes, I am delicate.
It is my strongest virtue
        to be torn to pieces,
        and grow back with delicacy,
        and grow back with poise,
        and to say that I know what it feels like to die.

        But life is where the living and the loving is,
        so that is where I choose to be.

You are delicate too, *deliciae.*

I just glued
all of the pieces
back together.

Please,
be gentle.

You are not the star
of my poems anymore.

This is how you know
I have let you go.

The rush
of passion,
of love,
of words,
through my veins.

That is why.

Just think
of how much power
one has to hold
to shake the world
with silence.

Poetry has made me brighter.

Poetry has made days
that were already steeped in emotion
unbearably serene.

Poetry has drenched me in empathy.
Poetry has made me softer.
Poetry has made me sit in rainstorms.

Poetry has made me appreciate
the perfect color of coffee.

Poetry has made me halt in chaos
and run when the world was still.

Poetry has made me grow into a person
with eyes I can look into,
and love.

Poetry is leading me home.

At first the light will feel like it is blinding
because darkness has surrounded you for so long.

I promise, *deliciae,*
after the stinging subsides,
you will finally be able to see that
      you are standing at the end
      of one of those tunnels
      people are always talking about.

It feels wrong
to come out of a war
without a scratch on my body
to show for it.

If anyone is so inclined
to see my scars,
look at any part of me
that can't be physically touched.

The wounds go on for miles,
but at the end,
I think there is light
and I know
there is healing.